Karate
Winning Kumite

Karate
Winning Kumite

Kunio Miyake & Jose M. Fraguas

EMPIRE Books
P.O. Box 491788, Los Angeles, CA 90049

Disclaimer
Please note that the author and publisher of this book are NOT RESPONSIBLE in any manner whatsoever for any injury that may result from practicing the techniques and/or following the instructions given within. Since the physical activities described herein may be too strenuous in nature for some readers to engage in safely, it is essential that a physician be consulted prior to training.

First published in 2006 by Empire Books
Copyright © 2006 by Empire Books

First edition
06 05 04 03 02 01 00 99 98 97 1 3 5 7 9 10 8 6 4 2
Printed in the United States of America.

Empire Books
P.O. Box 491788
Los Angeles, CA 90049

Library of Congress: 2006009386
ISBN-10: 1-933901-10-1
ISBN-13: 978-1-933901-10-7

Library of Congress Cataloging-in-Publication Data

Miyake, Kunio, 1946-
   Karate : winning kumite / by Kunio Miyake and Jose M. Fraguas. -- 1st ed.
      p. cm.
   Includes index.
   ISBN 1-933901-10-1 (pbk. : alk. paper)
   1. Karate. 2. Karate--Training. I. Fraguas, Jose M. II. Title.

GV1114.3.M597 2006
796.815'3--dc22
                    2006009386

Dedication

This book is dedicated to you—the karate practitioner. Your discipline, passion, and dedication to the art of karate served as the inspiration we drew upon to create the best book we could.

—The Authors

Acknowledgments

Many people were responsible for making this book possible, some more directly than others. We want to extend our gratitude to all those who so generously contributed their time and experience to the preparation of this work. A special thanks to designer Patrick Gross, and finally to our families, whose discernment is always tempered with kindness.

A word of appreciation is also due to Bill Bly, editor of *American Samurai* magazine, for his generosity in supplying great photographic material for some of the chapters. Without his support, this book would not exist.

You all have our enduring thanks.

—Kunio Miyake & Jose M. Fraguas

About the Authors

Kunio Miyake

Born in 1946, Miyake Sensei began teaching the martial arts in Japan. At the same time, he was teaching modern Japanese language and literature at the high school level. He moved to the United States in 1985 and—with permission from Shuko-kai Tani-ha Shito-Ryu and Soke Chojiro Tani—quickly established Shuko-Kai U.S.A. in Southern California. Founder of Shuko-kai International, Miyake Sensei currently holds an official U.S.A. National Karate-Do Federation 8th degree in karate-do and a 6th degree in shorinji aiki jiu-jitsu. The All-Japan Karate-do Federation and the World Shorinji Kempo Federation issued his instructor's licenses. Both associations require the highest caliber of karate and jiu-jitsu knowledge. In 1982, he was the All-Japan champion in Shito-Ryu Shuko-Kai and the 1988 U.S.A. Karate Federation National Champion. With many years of experience in the arts of Budo, Miyake Sensei is considered one of the most knowledgeable instructors in the kumite aspect of karate: "Modern kumite does not show the characteristics of each style anymore because everything is extremely unified in movement and approach," he says. "This is the result of sport competition. Back then, shotokan used *zenkutsu-dachi* and goju-ryu used *nekoashi-dachi* in kumite so you could tell the practitioner's style by just looking at the way he fought. Because karate now has a sport aspect, it has developed in a more modern and scientific approach to combat. Nowadays, we have only two styles for kumite: Japanese and rest of the world. And even the Japanese are changing to better accommodate the sportive approach." Miyake Sensei has earned a high level of respect by sharing karate-do with love, empathy and dedication. He strives for a life of tranquility and contentment, refreshed by the satisfaction derived from pursuing the way of karate with discipline and commitment.

Today he makes his home in Texas.

Jose M. Fraguas

Born and raised in Madrid, Spain, Jose M. Fraguas began his martial arts studies in grade school at age 9. He studied shito-ryu karate under Japanese Masters Masahiro Okada and Yashunari Ishimi, eventually receiving a fifth-degree black belt and the title of *Shihan* from Soke Mabuni Kenzo. He began his career as a writer at age 16 as a regular contributor to martial arts magazines in Great Britain, France, Spain, Italy, Germany, Portugal, Holland, and Australia.

In 1980, he moved to Los Angeles, California, where his open-minded mentality helped him to develop a realistic approach to the martial arts. After winning several national titles in both kata and kumite, he quit sport competition and began to supplement his previous training; he researched other disciplines such as Gracie jiu-jitsu and muay Thai.

Steeped in tradition yet looking to the future, Fraguas understands and appreciates martial arts history and philosophy and feels this rich heritage is a necessary steppingstone to personal growth and spiritual evolution. His desire to promote both ancient philosophy and modern thinking provided the motivation for writing one of the most acclaimed series of books in the art of karate-do, *"Karate Masters,"* which is comprised of three separate volumes. "If the motivation is just money, a book cannot be of good quality," Fraguas says. "If the book is written to just make people happy, it cannot be deep. I want to write books so I can learn as well as teach. Karate-do, like human life itself, is filled with experiences that seem quite ordinary at the time and assume a fabled stature only with the passage of the years. I hope this work will be appreciated by future practitioners of the art of karate."

Jose is currently living in Los Angeles, California. He can be contacted at *mastersseries@yahoo.com*.

Introduction

Kumite is one of the three fundamental training methods used in the art of karate-do. Unlike *kihon* and *kata* training, the element of kumite requires a direct and alive interaction with an opponent. Kumite is the ultimate test of the effectiveness of the techniques practiced in class. Free-sparring, although it is something that captures the attention of the practitioner from the very first day of training, is not something that should be addressed without the proper and correct preparation. Injuries, due to the lack of proper training and practice progression, are responsible for many talented karate-ka abandoning the art before they can actually reach their highest potential. The Nietzchean philosophy of "what doesn't kill you makes you stronger" doesn't really apply here and shouldn't be used as a motto for training. A proper progression in kumite is necessary to take the fighter from a white belt to the elite competition of a world championship.

Distance, timing and rhythm are the most important sparring principles in karate. The traditional [kumite] progression in the art provides a series of steppingstones before reaching the level of *jyu-kimute* or free-sparring. Although the format changes according to schools and teachers, those mentioned here are the basics for any training suitable for beginners.

Ippon Kumite (One-Step Sparring): This form of sparring is based on a pre-arranged set of one attack, one defense and one counterattack. It is a controlled sparring drill and helps a student sharpen reflexes, develop a sense of distance [*maai*] and establish proper technical form. The time between blocks and counterattacks are more prevalent

here. The attacker reduces the telegraphing of intent to attack and the defender has to react faster.

Sanbon Kumite (Three-Step Sparring): This form of sparring follows the format of ippon kumite, but it requires the attacker to deliver three different attacks that the defender should block. Only after the last attack can the defender apply his counterattack. It is important here to keep the center of gravity in place while retreating. The three attacks enable the practitioner to incorporate different rhythms into the offensive actions. For instance: 1-2, 3 or 1, 2-3.

Gohon Kumite (Five-Step Sparring): This follows the format of the previous drills but the number of attacks is increased to five. The counterattack is only permitted after the last offensive move of the attacker. Although it is mentioned here at the end, gohon kumite is usually the first kind of sparring because it teaches a practitioner to time the blocks with the attacks in a sequence. The student learns proper distancing and correct posture under attacking circumstances.

Although these three basic sparring drills seem to be very easy, it is important to understand that when properly done they can be extremely challenging and even dangerous. The attack should be initiated from a real striking distance. And the timing of the defender in blocking the attacks should be precise and the retreating footwork should only start after the attacker has actually initiated the offense. At a more advanced level, the instructor will introduce the element of *jyu* or "free," which forces the defender to be prepared for any kind of attack [*tsuki* or *keri*] at any level [*gedan, chudan* or *jodan*]. Once the student has achieved proficiency in controlling attacks and defenses using the proper judgment of distance, timing and rhythm, he will be introduced to *jyu-kumite*, which actually is free-sparring and the final form of kumite. At this stage, the karate-ka is capable of judging distance, applying offensive and defensive movements at will and of controlling his own attacks. The competitor should stick to the basics as learned in kihon, but it is true that these fundamental techniques are slightly altered to better fit the requirements of the actual sparring. It is important to maintain the intrinsic principles of power direction and technical delivery even if the original form is altered. Due to this fact, kihon kumite has become a topic of discussion. This is form of kumite in which the techniques are performed in a more kumite or sparring format and in which elements like *hiki-te*, perfect stance and similar aspects are substituted by speed, mobility and explosiveness in search of efficiency in a real encounter against an alive opponent. The techniques used in this kind of training are comprised of basic movements (*mae-tsuki, gyaku-tsuki, ura-ken, mae-geri, mawashi-geri*, et cetera) because those are the ones mostly used in competition. They are trained in combinations (*renraku waza*) and incorporate a more mobile footwork pattern that perfectly fits the rigors of elite competition. Mobility is the key element in sparring and competition. The use of proper footwork will allow the com-

petitor to be in distance, out of distance, to close the distance or to create distance to avoid an attack. Therefore, it is important that all karate-ka pay the necessary attention to develop clean and precise footwork patterns that deliver the punches and kicks to the target. It is imperative to rely on mobility and skill to determine the judgment of distance. Regardless of how good a competitor may be in judging the punching and kicking distance for punching and kicking techniques— if he doesn't have proper footwork—the best technique in the world will be useless. He won't be able to reach his opponent nor will he be able to avoid any attack. The quality of a karate-ka's techniques depends on his footwork. Footwork and distance control go hand-in-hand. When practicing kihon, the element of distance is not present. Distance is incorporated when the practitioner starts training in any form of kumite in which a live opponent is an integral part of the action. There are some fundamental principles all competitors should keep in mind when practicing kumite.

Distance in Attack

- Always use an economical initiation for any movement. Don't telegraph intentions.
- A proper kamae allows a karate-ka to move economically and without disturbing his position. This principle facilitates freedom of movement.
- Keep shifting footwork in order to have the correct distance measure.
- Always recover to kamae after the attack. Keep good balance and posture with zanchin after delivering the technique.

Distance in Defense

- Have a good judgment of the opponent's length of penetration. Feel how deep he can go with his attack.
- Develop a sense of spatial perception or aura related to the opponent's movements.
- Always use the proper *kamae* for correct defenses and counterattacks.
- Maintain at all times the correct body balance when reacting to the opponent's attack.

Perfect timing, the most difficult principle of combat, depends on the competitor's proper sense of distancing. It is the third building block and the one which actually involves the striking limbs (arms and legs) of the karate-ka. A punch delivered at the wrong time (too soon or too late) will either lack of its full power or will never reach the target. The perfect technique always "fits" into the space created between the karate-ka and his opponent as a hand slips in a perfect size glove ... with no extra spaces. The best way to develop timing is through an extensive and diligent training of sparring drills with a partner.

Other more advanced principles and elements of combat deal with rhythm, broken rhythm, feints and the always necessary tactics and strategies (*go no sen* and *sen no sen*, direct and indirect attacks, attacks by drawing, progressive indirect attacks, attacks by combination, et cetera) that allow the competitor to take advantages of the mental and psychological aspects of kumite. Ultimately, it is the karate-ka. He is the one who has to put all the technical and mental elements of combat together to create his own style of kumite. It should be remembered at all times that any technique should display the proper attributes of a real karate movement. Regardless of the competitor's technical preferences, elements such as kamae (ready position), kime (focus), zanchin (total awareness), kokyo (breath control), et cetera must part an integral part of the physical action. Competition is a challenging test for the practitioner's skill. In a traditional way, the training of karate-do is like forging a sword. As the old masters knew, the true sword's worth can only be known by testing it in combat.

KAMAE

The kamae position should be the most favorable to the mechanical execution of all the techniques the fighter has. Kamae is described as a posture or stance. It includes not only the position of the arms and legs, the body angle and center of gravity, it often implies a mindset as well. There is an important parallel in karate between one's physical and one's psychological bearing. A strong physical stance helps promote the correlative adoption of a strong physical attitude that is extremely important in a fighting situation.

KAMAE: THE ON-GUARD POSITION

Photo 1—Correct

The trunk must be straight in a vertical position. This is controlled primarily by the position of the leading foot and leg. The hands cover the center of the body, relaxed and ready to attack or defend. The weight is evenly distributed on both feet, ever ready to pull the trigger into action. The position should provide a maximum of relaxation combined with smoothness of movement at all times.

Photo 2—Correct

Maintain the verticality of the body at all times. Don't bring your hands too close to the body and keep them moving frequently without creating unnecessary opening in your guard. Keep your body weight on the balls of your feet to facilitate smooth footwork and mobility in your actions. Balance is the most important consideration in kamae. The lead foot should be hampered as little as possible to facilitate the movement in attack.

Photo A—Incorrect—FRONT VIEW

This photo shows the most common mistakes in kamae:

- The hands are too far apart, creating an opening for a direct attack.
- The stance is too wide, which prevents the fighter from using smooth footwork and makes him vulnerable to sweeping techniques.
- The trunk leans to the back, which delays movement and warns the opponent of any attacking intention, since it will be necessary to transfer the body weight before starting the attack.
- The rear leg is too stiff. The heel of the back leg should be slightly raised and not fully planted with all the body weight on it.

Photo B—Incorrect—SIDE VIEW

From a side view we can see:

- The excessive length of the stance.
- The excessive opening in the guard.
- The center of gravity leaning backwards.

BASIC TECHNIQUES

Competition karate relies on a limited number of techniques that have been proven useful and effective in sport tournaments. The simpler and more direct the technique is, the more chances we'll have to score with it. Try to keep you techniques direct and simple, but with a sophisticated use of such other fighting elements as strategy, timing, distance, and rhythm. The highest level of sophistication in combat lies in simplicity.

KIZAME-TSUKI (Jabbing Punch)

Kizame-tsuki is a short, jabbing punch delivered with the front hand **(A)**. It is a fast movement and is used with many different purposes. It may be used as a stunning technique to set up a following attack in the form of a feint—when taking the initiative, or it may be used as a stopping action when defending an attack from the opponent, surprising him at the moment he tries to close the distance.

The body remains in a 45-degree angle [hammi] to avoid any incoming attacks [when defending] or to reduce the target areas of our own body when attacking **(B).** The delivery action for this technique is shorter but faster than any other punch in karate-do. When used as a feint, it works perfectly in combination with a gyaku-tsuki.

There are four important aspects to this technique:
- Move the lead foot towards the opponent.
- Always hit with the hand of the same side your lead is moving.
- Use the technique in medium range.
- Do not move the upper body or lean it forward. Keep the body straight and use the 'hara' to create momentum and energy in the action.

TIP: Always remember to move your body weight into the punch, and use the hip turn to add 'snap' to your technique. It is important to synchronize the step, the hip turn, and the snap of the shoulder to achieve maximum power at the moment of impact.

Miyake Sensei faces his opponent **(1)**. He steps in and delivers a kizame-tsuki to the opponent's face **(2)**. Then, he retreats to kamae. Zanchin **(3)**.

GYAKU-TSUKI (Reverse Punch)

Gyaku-tsuki is one of the most frequently used hand attacks in the art of karate-do **(A)**. It is a very powerful punch and, due to its versatility, the most used in sport competition. It can be used in an offensive action—as a direct attack or in combination, or with a defensive approach as a counter to any incoming attack.

The hips from a 'hammi' position, should turn completely toward the opponent **(B)**. This is essential when executing this punching technique. The hips should rotate so that they are square-on to the front on completion.

- Stability of the legs is essential. The hip movement must be powerful and precise, without compromising the balance of the body.
- Do not lean forward. Although this would add 'reach' to the punch, it definitely would weaken the power, due to the inability to contract the abdomen properly at the moment of impact.
- The beginning of the technique starts with the movement of the hip; only then does the arm begin to move. These two elements are combined in one single sequence, but they should not be mistaken as 'one single action.'
- Relax the shoulder of the punching arm. It should be at the same level as the other shoulder. The muscle contraction takes effect in the latissimus dorsis and not in the shoulder.

TIP: A 'push' of the rear leg should be added to the momentum generated by the turn of the hips, to generate additional force by bringing the center of gravity forward. Always keep the hips at the same level.

Miyake Sensei faces his opponent **(1)**. He steps-in with his right leg and delivers a reverse punch to the opponent mid-section **(2)**. Then, he retreats to kamae. Zanchin **(3)**.

Kicking Techniques

The kicking techniques for sport competition are based on modified approaches of the basic and fundamental ways of delivering the techniques in kihon. The main and most important change is found in the hiki-ashi phase of all the kicks. While the hiki-ashi [preparatory chambering position of the knee] varies for each kick in a fundamental kihon practice, for sport competition the main idea is to use the same 'preparatory phase' for all major kicking techniques. In this way, it will be more difficult for the opponent to 'read' what type of kick we are using in our attack

(Front View A & B).
From a kamae position **(A)**, the knee is brought straight up front **(B)**. It is from that 'neutral' chambering position that all the three major kicking techniques should be delivered:

- Front kick (Mae-geri) **(1)**
- Roundhouse kick (Mawashi-geri) **(2)**
- Hook kick (Ura Mawashi-geri) **(3)**

TIP: Always lift the leg high and bend the knee fully in the preparatory stage of the kick.

- The hip and thigh muscles are very important in any kicking technique; therefore, maintain a strong and solid connection with the pelvis by keeping the hips stable. The supporting leg should be slightly tense and bent at the knee level.

Front View A   **Front View B**

Front Kick (1)

The kick is delivered by straightening the knee in a direct line with the center of the body, and keeping the back upright. It is a very direct and simple kick, but extremely hard to use properly. Due to its simplicity, a perfect sense of timing and opportunity are necessary to score with it.

Roundhouse Kick (2)

This kick is delivered by using a powerful snap of the hips and a solid pivot of the foot of the supporting leg. The knee should be kept straight, allowing the lower part of the leg to hit the target in a circular motion.

Hook Kick (3)

The hook kick follows an arc across the front of the body and out to the side. It requires a powerful movement of the hips and a strong pivot of the foot of the supporting leg. This technique may appear weak, but it is very effective in a punch-kick combination and as a counter to many punching attacks to chudan (medium) level.

FOOTWORK

The quality of a karateka's technique will depend on his ability to use the footwork. If his footwork is slow, his punches and kicks also will be slow. Proper use of footwork and correct mobility always precede the speed of punches and kicks. Any sparring match is a matter of motion, and the proper footwork can beat any punch or kick. The more adept the fighter is at the correct use of footwork, the less he will have to use his arms to avoid being hit. Aim always for simplification in the use of footwork patterns. Use them as a means of deception, and remember that the essence of fighting is the art of moving.

ADVANCING SLIDE AND STEP

From an on-guard stance **(1)**, move the rear foot close to the lead foot without changing the level of the hips **(2)**. Now, take a step with the lead foot forward and adopt the on-guard stance again **(3)**.

TIP: Maintain the knee of the front leg slightly bent so you can keep the hips at the same height level. Do not move the trunk during the footwork action.

ADVANCING STEP-AND-SLIDE

From an on-guard stance **(1)**, take a step forward with your front foot **(2)**. Bring the rear foot to the front, covering the same distance the front foot gained in the previous step **(3)**.

TIP: A correct distribution of weight on both legs will make for perfect balance. Lighten the stance so there will be less force of inertia to overcome.

RETREATING SLIDE-AND-STEP

The principle is the same as in the Advancing Step-and-Slide, but moving backwards. From an on-guard position **(1)**, slide your front foot back close to the rear foot **(2)**, and immediately move the rear foot back the same distance that was covered by the front foot **(3)**.

TIP: Remember that both feet are on the floor at all times, and the slide-and-step should be done without disturbing the kamae.

RETREATING STEP-AND-SLIDE
From an on-guard stance **(1)**, take a step back with the rear foot **(2)**, and then slide the front foot back to assume the kamae position again **(3)**.

TIP: The body maintains the fundamental position throughout. Be aware that, since this is a defensive maneuver to avoid an attack, a possible counterattack can be executed in step #2.

FULL STEP FORWARD

From an on-guard position **(1)**, bring the rear foot next to the front foot **(2)**, and take a forward step with the same foot **(3)**.

TIP: This type of footwork is used in long distance attacks, and although one foot may not be touching the floor, the hips must be at the same height level all the time.

FULL STEP BACKWARD

This principle is the same as the Full Step Forward, but retreating. From an on-guard position **(1)**, bring the front foot close to the rear foot **(2)**, and take a step back with the same foot **(3)**.

TIP: Maintain the weight on the initial rear leg, since it will be the support throughout the whole motion and the first line of defense if attacked during the retreat. Make the step backward with the line of engagement well covered.

SIDESTEP TO THE RIGHT

From an on-guard position **(1)**, move your rear foot to the right side about half of your shoulder width **(2)**. Immediately move your front foot and readjust the stance **(3)**.

TIP: Never step in a way that that you would cross your feet. When facing an opponent on Ai-hammi, this is the safest footwork to counter any attack executed by the opponent's rear hand and leg.

SIDESTEP TO THE LEFT

From an on-guard position **(1)**, move the rear foot to the left side about half of your shoulder width, but make sure it is not in line with the front foot **(2)**. Then move your front foot to the left side to readjust the stance **(3)**.

TIP: This footwork pattern should be executed carefully, with a small step by the rear foot. It is more difficult but safer than stepping to the right, and therefore, should be used more often.

ANGLE-IN TO THE RIGHT

From an on-guard position **(1)**, move the rear foot to the side and adopt a 45-degree angle stance **(2)**. Return to the original front stance **(3)**.

TIP: The height and distance of the front leg and hip should remain constant throughout the whole movement.

ANGLE-IN TO THE LEFT
From an on-guard position
(1), move the rear foot to the
side as you pivot over the
front foot **(2)**. Then return to
the original stance by bringing
the rear foot back **(3)**.

TIP: The body should move
like the fulcrum of a door. This
movement is especially useful
to avoid frontal attacks and
effectively counter from within
a distance.

STEP AND SLIDE

Miyake Sensei faces his opponent (1). He closes the distance and scores with a gyaku-tsuki by using the step-and-slide footwork (2). With the step, he closes the gap between him and his opponent, and with the final sliding movement of his rear foot, he brings the momentum from his body into the punch.

TIP: It is important not to 'jump' with the lead foot but 'slide' smoothly into the target.

2

SLIDE-AND-STEP

Miyake Sensei squares off against his opponent **(1)**. Miyake brings his rear foot close to his left **(2),** and explodes into a powerful step forward with his left leg to close the distance with his opponent, then scores with a right reverse punch to the mid-section **(3)**.

TIP: The movement ot the rear leg should be smooth and deceptive, since the opponent can 'read' the attack by detecting the action of the leg. Keep the height of your hip at the same level throughout the whole movement.

FULL FORWARD STEP

From an on-guard [kamae] position **(1)**, Miyake Sensei takes a full step forward and scores with oi-tsuki jodan **(2)**.

TIP: Remember to use the front leg as 'traction' to pull your body forward. The secret lies in using the hips to deliver the punch, not the real leg. Make sure you fist hits the target before the moving foot lands in front of the opponent. This way the body weight will be transferred to the arm and not to the ground. Maintain a minimum of movement in the upper body when taking the step forward. Any unnecessary body movement will telegraph the attack.

RETREAT AND PUSH SHUFFLE

Miyake Sensei faces his opponent **(1)**. When the opponent steps in to close the distance and attack with a gyaku-tsuki, Miyake Sensei slides his lead foot back enough to make the opponent's punch fall short without moving his rear foot **(2)**, and immediately pushes forward to score with a reverse punch to the face **(3)**.

TIP: Do not move the rear foot when sliding the front foot back. This will allow you to maintain the exact distance to score with your technique once you push forward with explosiveness.

STEP BACK

Miyake Sensei squares off against his opponent **(1)**. When the opponent closes the distance and attacks with a reverse punch, Miyake moves his rear foot back enough to drop his body and create additional distance that make the opponent's punch fall short by one inch **(2)**. As the opponent's attack fails, Miyake simply brings his rear foot forward and counterattacks with haito-uchi to the temple **(3)**.

TIP: Since the front foot is not moving in this technique, the distance judgment has to be very precise. By moving the rear foot, we create the necessary 'extra' inch to make the opponent's attack fail while we still are 'in distance' to score with a counter.

SIDE STEP & BODY TURN

Miyake Sensei faces his opponent **(1)**. When the opponent closes the distance and attacks with a reverse punch, Miyake moves his rear foot backward and turns his hips slightly to the side **(2)**, following with a mae-tsuki to the opponent's face **(3)**.

TIP: Make sure the rear foot moves simultaneously with your hip. Otherwise, the opponent's punch will connect with your body since, although the leg will be in motion, the body will stay in the same place.

REPLACEMENT STEP

Miyake Sensei squares off against his opponent **(1).** When the opponent closes the distance and attacks with a reverse punch, Miyake brings his left foot back together with his right, as he simultaneously deflects the attack **(2).** Then he steps forward with his right foot, replacing the left foot, and scores with a mae-tsuki to the face **(3).**

TIP: Since the distance between your body and the maximum extension of the opponent's tack should be very short, make sure your blocking hand is secure, deflecting the attack. Then explode with a counter-punch.

KUMITE COMBINATIONS

I n this chapter, we'll analyze many of the most frequently used fighting combinations in tournament karate. A precise sense of timing, distance, and rhythm is necessary to master these combinations. All of them are simple and direct. They are presented in a systematic approach to applied kumite that is designed to provide a guide for sport and tournament sparring. Practice these techniques until your ability to react and respond becomes second nature.

Miyake Sensei facing his opponent **(1)**. The opponent attacks with gyaku-tsuki chudan that Miyake intercepts with his right hand **(2)**. Then the opponent punches with his right hand to the face, but Miyake blocks it again with the same hand **(3)**, to counter-attack with a reverse punch to the midsection **(4)**.

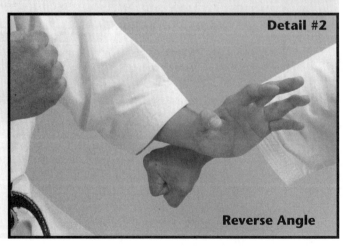

Detail #2

Reverse Angle

3

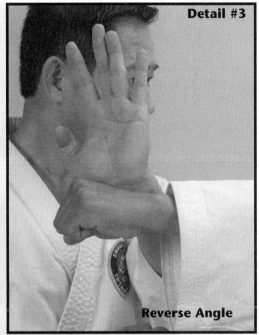

Detail #3

Reverse Angle

4

Miyake Sensei squares off against his opponent **(1)**. The opponent attacks with a jodan tsuki that is blocked by Miyake's left hand **(2)**.

Detail #2

The opponent continues his attack with a gyaku-tsuki chudan **(3)**, which is parried by Miyake's left hand **(4)**. Then Miyake counterattacks with a reverse punch to the face **(5)**.

Detail #4

Sensei faces his opponent **(1)**. Miyake parries his opponent's attack, using his left hand **(2)**. Then, he uses his right hand to stop the opponent's gyaku-tsuki **(3)**, and follows up with a backfist to the temple **(4)**.

Detail #2

3

Detail #3

4

Sensei squares off against his opponent **(1)**. The opponent attacks with a front kick to the midsection that is blocked by Sensei's right hand **(2)**.

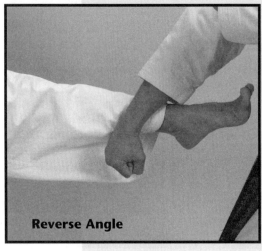

Reverse Angle

Detail #2

Immediately, the attacker throws a jodan mae-tsuki to the face that Miyake
intercepts with his right hand **(3)**; then he counterattacks with a left punch
to the opponent's face **(4)**.

Reverse Angle

Detail #3

Miyake Sensei faces his opponent **(1)**. The opponent attacks with a jodan mawashi-geri that is blocked by Sensei's left hand **(2)**. The opponent continues his attacking combination with a reverse punch to the stomach that is blocked by Miyake's left hand **(3)**. Then Miyake counterattacks with a haito-uchi to the temple **(4)**.

Detail #2

3

Detail #3

4

Sensei faces his opponent **(1)**. The opponent closes the distance and attacks with a gyaku-tsuki jodan that is blocked by Miyake's right hand **(2)**. The opponent steps in and throws another gyaku-tsuki with the right hand, which forces Miyake Sensei to step back to block the attack with his left hand **(3)**. After a quick adjustment of the distance, Miyake counterattacks with a gyaku-tsuki to the face **(4)**.

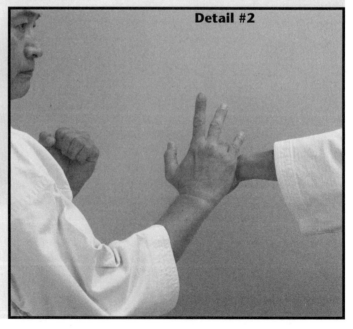

Detail #2

Detail #3

Miyake faces his opponent **(1)**. The opponent attacks, using a mae-tsuki jodan that is blocked by Sensei's right hand **(2)**. Then, the opponent steps in with an oi-tsuki jodan that is parried by Miyake, who then uses his left hand **(3)** to immediately counter with a front punch of his right hand to the opponent's face **(4)**.

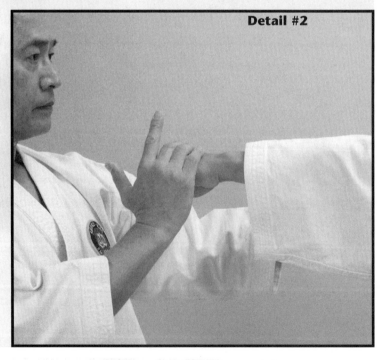

Detail #2

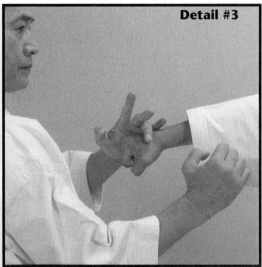

Miyake Sensei squares against his opponent **(1)**. The opponent attacks with a punch to the face that is blocked by Sensei's left hand **(2)**. The opponent follows with a gyaku-tsuki chudan that is blocked by Miyake's right hand **(3)**. By angling his body, Miyake creates distance and counter-attacks with uraken [backfist] to the face **(4)**.

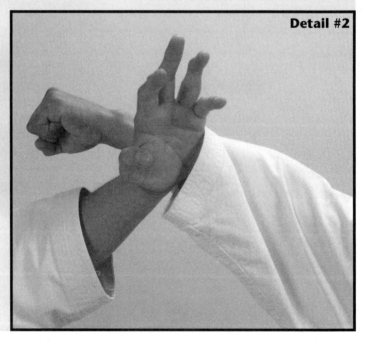

Detail #2

3

Detail #3

4

Miyake Sensei faces his opponent **(1)**. The opponent attacks with a left hand punch to the face that Miyake blocks with the outside part of his left hand **(2)**. Then he steps in and scores with gyaku-tsuki to the mid-section **(3)**.

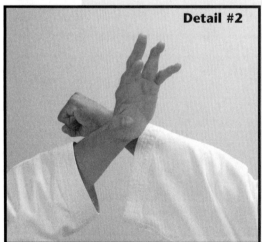

Detail #2

Miyake Sensei faces his opponent **(1)**. Sensei closes the distance and attacks with a reverse punch that falls short **(2)**. Then he changes his body level and scores with a clean kizame-tsuki to the face **(3)**. Retreat to kamae. Zanchin **(4)**.

Sensei faces his opponent **(1)**. The opponent closes the distance and attacks with mae-tsuki to the face that falls short, due to the retreat of Miyake **(2)**. The opponent regroups **(3)**, and launches a new attack that is blocked by Miyake's left hand **(4)**.

When the opponent continues the attacking combination with a reverse punch to the midsection, Sensei blocks it with his left hand **(5)**, and counters with a right gyaku-tsuki to the chest **(6)**.

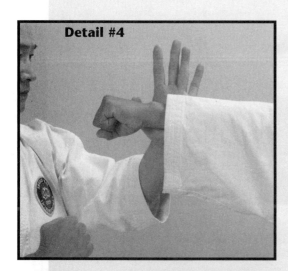

Miyake Sensei squares off against his opponent **(1)**. Miyake initiates his movement to close the distance **(2)**, and steps in to punch his opponent in the face with oi-tsuki **(3)**, followed by a reverse punch to the midsection **(4)**. Retreat to kamae. Zanchin **(5)**.

Miyake Sensei faces his opponent **(1)**. He steps in and scores directly with a mae-tsuki jodan **(2)**, followed by a reverse punch to the stomach **(3)**. Return to kamae. Zanchin **(4)**.

Sensei squares off against his opponent **(1)**. Miyake uses a direct angle of attack to score with a mae-geri chudan **(2)**, followed by a right punch to the face **(3)**. Retreat to kamae. Zanchin **(4)**.

Miyake Sensei faces his opponent **(1)**. Sensei brings his right foot close to his left to close the distance **(2)**, brings his left knee up into hiki-ashi **(3)**, and throws a roundhouse kick to the face **(4)**, followed by a right reverse punch to the stomach **(5)**. Retreat to kamae. Zanchin **(6)**.

Miyake Sensei squares off against his opponent **(1)**. Sensei closes the distance by checking his opponent's left hand **(2)**, and follows with gyaku-tsuki jodan **(3)**.

Then Miyake steps in and throws a reverse punch to the midsection **(4)**.
Retreat to kamae. Zanchin **(5)**.

Sensei squares off against his opponent **(1)**. Miyake closes the distance and attacks with a straight punch to the face **(2)**, followed by oi-tsuki jodan **(3)**. Retreat to kamae. Zanchin **(4)**.

Miyake Sensei faces his opponent **(1)**. Miyake closes the distance and attacks with a left hand punch to the face **(2)**, followed by a reverse punch to the midsection **(3)**, and a mae-tsuki jodan **(4)**. Retreat to kamae. Zanchin **(5)**.

Miyake Sensei squares off against his opponent **(1)**. He closes the distance and throws a front punch to the face that falls short **(2)**.

Miyake regroups his position **(3)** and initiates a new attack with a mae-tsuki jodan **(4)**, followed by a gyaku-tsuki to the midsection **(5)**. Retreat to kamae. Zanchin **(6)**.

Miyake Sensei faces his opponent **(1)**. Sensei attacks with a left punch to the face **(2)** and a gyaku-tsuki to the midsection **(3)**, followed by a step in with the right foot and a left hand reverse punch to the stomach **(4)**. Retreat to kamae. Zanchin **(5)**.

Sensei squares off against his opponent **(1)**.

Miyake closes the distance using his left hand to feint and open the angle
(2) for a front kick to the midsection **(3)**, followed by a mae-tsuki to the
face **(4)**. Retreat to kamae. Zanchin **(5)**.

Miyake Sensei faces his opponent **(1)**. He uses his left hand punch to feint and cover his entry **(2)** with his right foot **(3)**,

to throw a left roundhouse kick to the face **(4)**, followed by a reverse punch to the midsection **(5)**. Retreat to kamae. Zanchin **(6)**.

Miyake faces his opponent **(1)**. He uses his left hand to check the opponent's lead hand, and attacks with a jodan gyaku-tsuki that the opponent nullifies by stepping back **(2)**. Then, Miyake steps in and attacks with a left reverse punch **(3)**, followed by a front kick to the stomach **(4)**.

Kuzushi

Kuzushi is the act of disturbing or breaking an opponent's posture or balance, forcing him to lose his balance through a shift of his center of gravity before committing himself to the actual attack. Ideally, we should be able to turn our own attacking force against the opponent. (Sen-no-sen). Sometimes it is necessary to use one's own force (Go-no-sen) to achieve this, and sometimes a combination of the two methods may be used. This is a way to maneuver oneself into a position from which a throwing action can be conveniently executed, before one obtains a good Kuzushi.

Miyake Sensei squares off against his opponent **(1)**. The opponent closes the distance and attacks with a punch to the face. Miyake steps back and uses his left foot **(2)** to sweep the inside of his opponent's left leg **(3)**, bringing him down to the ground to score the final punch **(4)**.

Miyake faces his opponent **(1)**. When the opponent closes the distance to attack with a punch, Miyake parries the attack with his right hand and sweeps his opponent with his right leg **(2)**, bringing him down to the ground **(3)**, where he finalizes the counterattack with a punch to the midsection **(4)**.

Miyake Sensei squares off against his opponent **(1)**. Miyake closes the distance and checks the opponent's lead hand with his left hand **(2)**. Then he steps in with his right leg **(3)** and turns his body to the right **(4)**, which brings his opponent to the ground **(5)**, where Miyake finishes the aggressor **(6)** with a punch to the face **(7)**.

Detail #2

Reverse Angle

Reverse Angle

Miyake Sensei faces his opponent **(1)**. Miyake brings his left foot to his right and covers his entry by checking his opponent's right hand **(2)**,

enabling him to throw a roundhouse kick to the face with the right leg **(3)**, followed by an outside sweep to the back of the opponent's right knee **(4)**, which brings him to the ground **(5)**, where Miyake finishes him off with a punch to the stomach **(6)**.

Miyake squares off against his opponent **(1)**. He enters and pushes his opponent's left arm up **(2)**, to open space so he can bring his right leg behind the opponent **(3)**. Using his thigh **(4)**, he brings his opponent off balance **(5 & 6)**, and to the ground **(7)**, where Miyake finishes him off with a punch to the face **(8)**.

6

Reverse Angle

7

8

SANBON
TO KUZUSHI

I n this chapter, the important elements that we have developed in Sanbon Kumite, such as good balance in successive combinations and proper sense of distance, are combined with the close-range techniques of Kuzushi. We'll be using the initial techniques to 'open' the door to throw the opponent onto the ground and finish him off there. A deeper sense of timing and distance is require in these combinations since we are moving from a long or medium range to a close-quarter scenario when our body will be close to the opponent's.

Sensei faces his opponent **(1)**. The opponent attacks with a punch to the face that Miyake blocks with his left arm **(2)**. Then he counterattacks with a reverse punch to the midsection **(3)**. Retreat to kamae. Zanchin **(4)**.

Sensei faces his opponent **(1)**. The opponent attacks with a punch to the face that Miyake blocks with his left arm **(2)**. Using his right hand, he grabs the opponent's left arm **(3)** and, with his right foot, sweeps the opponent's left leg **(4 & 5)**.

Once the opponent is on the ground **(6)**, Miyake finishes him off with a
punch to the face **(7 & 8)**.

Miyake Sensei squares off against his opponent **(1)**. The opponent attacks with a gyaku-tsuki that Miyake blocks with his left hand **(2)**. Then, he counterattacks with a right reverse punch to the midsection **(3)**. Retreat to kamae. Zanchin **(4)**.

Miyake Sensei faces his opponent **(1)**. The opponent attacks with a reverse punch to the mid-section that Miuyake traps by using his two hands **(2)**. Then he applies a wrist lock **(3)** that brings the opponent to the ground **(4)**, where Miyake finishes him off with a punch to the stomach **(5)**.

Detail #2A

Reverse Angle

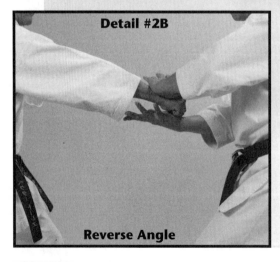

Detail #2B

Reverse Angle

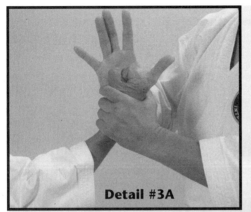

Detail #3A

Detail #3B

4

Reverse Angle

5

Reverse Angle

Miyake Sensei squares off against his opponent **(1)**. The opponent attacks with a front kick that is blocked by Miyake's gedan-barai **(2)**. Then Miyake follows with a reverse punch to the mid-section **(3)**. Retreat to kamae. Zanchin **(4)**.

Miyake Sensei faces his opponent **(1)**. The opponent attacks with a front kick to the stomach that is blocked by Miyake's left arm **(2)**. Miyake steps in with his right leg between his opponent's **(3)** and throws him onto to the ground **(4)**, where he applies a final punch to the midsection **(5)**.

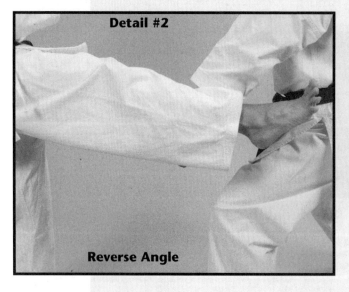

Detail #2

Reverse Angle

Detail #3A

Reverse Angle

Detail #3B

Reverse Angle

4

Reverse Angle

5

Reverse Angle

Miyake faces his opponent **(1)**. The opponent attacks with a right hand punch that is blocked by Miyake's left hand **(2)**. Then he follows the counterattack with a gyaku-tsuki to the stomach **(3)**. Retreat to kamae. Zanchin **(4)**.

Sensei Miyake squares off against his opponent **(1)**. The opponent attacks with a punch to the face that is blocked by Sensei's left hand **(2)**. Using his left hand, Miyake grabs his opponent's right arm **(3)** and turns his body to the side as he pulls the opponent's head down with his right hand **(4)**. This action brings the opponent off balance **(5)** and onto the ground **(6)**, where Miyake finishes him off with a punch to the midsection **(7)**.

Detail #2A
Reverse Angle

Detail #2B
Reverse Angle

Detail #3
Reverse Angle

Detail #4

Reverse Angle

Winning Kumite

Miyake Sensei faces his opponent **(1)**. The opponent attacks with a front kick to the stomach that is blocked by Sensei's left hand **(2 & 3)**.

Sensei's defensive block pushes the opponent's leg away **(4)**, opening an angle for a reverse punch to the back **(5)**. Retreat to kamae. Zanchin **(6)**.

Sensei squares off against his opponent **(1)**. The opponent attacks with a front kick to the stomach that Miyake Sensei deflects with sukui-uke **(2)**.

Then he grabs the opponent's shoulders from behind **(3)** and pulls him to the ground **(4)**, where he finishes him off with a punch to the stomach **(5)**.

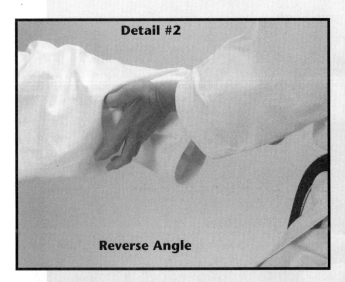

Detail #2

Reverse Angle

3

4

5

Sensei faces his opponent **(1)**. When the opponent attacks with a front kick, Miyake uses ude-uke to deflect the action **(2)**, which opens an angle to **(3)** counterattack with haito-uchi to the face **(4)**. Retreat to kamae. Zanchin **(5)**.

Sensei faces his opponent **(1)**. The opponent attacks with a front kick to the midsection that is blocked by Miyake's sukui-uke **(2)**. Then, Miyake grabs the opponent's kicking leg and controls the right shoulder by using his left hand **(3)**. Immediately, he sweeps the opponent's supporting leg with his left foot **(4)**, and brings him onto the ground **(5)**, where Miyake finishes him off with a punch to the stomach **(6)**.

Detail #3

4

Reverse Angle

5

Reverse Angle

6

Reverse Angle

Miyake Sensei squares off against his opponent **(1)**. The opponent attacks with a high roundhouse kick that Sensei deflects with a double block **(2)**.

Sensei's right hand 'hooks' the opponent's leg and pushes it away **(3)**, creating an opening for a punch to the head **(4)**. Retreat to kamae. Zanchin **(5)**.

Miyake squares off against his opponent **(1)**. The opponent attacks with a high roundhouse kick that Sensei deflects with a double block **(2)**. Sensei's right hand 'hooks' the opponent's leg **(3)** and traps it, applying a lock to the knee **(4)**, that brings the opponent to the ground **(5)**, where Miyake finishes him off with a punch to the back **(6)**.

Detail #2A

Detail #2B

Detail #3

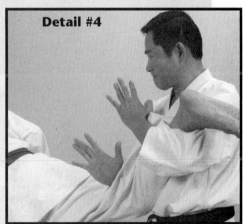

Detail #4

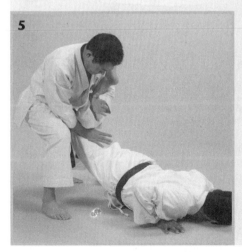

Miyake Sensei faces his opponent **(1)**. When the opponent throws a high roundhouse kick to the head, Miyake Sensei blocks the attack **(2)** and delivers a reverse punch to the stomach **(3)**. Retreat to kamae. Zanchin **(4)**.

Miyake Sensei squares off against his opponent **(1)**. The opponent attacks with a jodan mawashi-geri that is blocked by Miyake **(2)**, who immediately uses his left hand to push the opponent away and his right hand to grab and control the kicking leg **(3)**. Then he turns his body to the left **(4)**, unbalancing his opponent **(5)** and taking him to the ground, where Miyake finishes him off with a punch to the stomach **(6)**.

Detail #2

3

Detail #3

4

Detail #4

Front View

5

6

Sensei faces his opponent **(1)**. The opponent attacks with a front kick to the midsection that Miyake deflects by retreating with his right leg and blocking with his right hand **(2)**, before he launches a high roundhouse kick to the face as a counterattack **(3)**.

Miyake Sensei faces his opponent **(1)**. He blocks the opponent's front kick by using both hands and by retreating with his right leg to create distance **(2)**. Then, he steps in and brings his right leg inside his opponent's supporting leg **(3)**, as he simultaneously grabs the opponent's shoulder and turns him around **(4)** to bring him to the ground **(5)**, where he finishes him off **(6)**, with a punch to the stomach **(7)**.

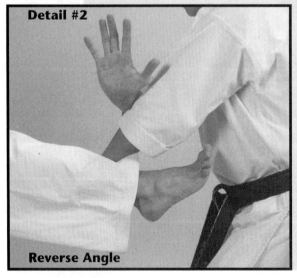

Detail #2

Reverse Angle

4

Detail #4A

Detail #4B

5

6

7

Miyake Sensei squares off against his opponent **(1)**. As soon as the opponent initiates a straight punch attack, Miyake angles his body in and counterattacks with a mae-tsuki to the face **(2)**. Retreat to kamae. Zanchin **(3)**

2

Detail #2

Back View

3

Miyake Sensei faces his opponent **(1)**. When the opponent tries to punch Miyake's face, Sensei brings his left arm up and blocks the action, as he simultaneously closes the distance with his left leg **(2)**. Then, he grabs the opponent's attacking arm and steps in with his right foot behind the opponent's left **(3)**. Miyake turns his body around and brings his opponent to the ground **(4)**, where he finishes him off with a punch to the stomach **(5)**.

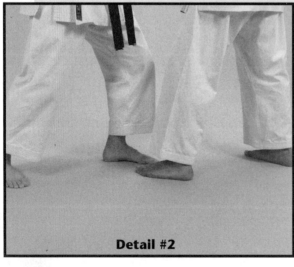

Detail #2

Detail #3A

Detail #3B

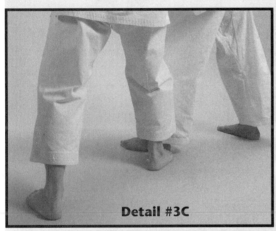

Detail #3C

4

5

Sensei faces his opponent **(1)**. When the opponent attacks with a gyaku-tsuki chudan, Sensei steps back and blocks with his left hand **(2)**. Then he follows with a reverse punch of his own to the stomach **(3)**. Retreat to kamae. Zanchin **(4)**.

Miyake Sensei faces his opponent **(1)**. When the opponent attacks with a gyaku-tsuki chudan, Sensei steps back and blocks with his left hand **(2)**. Then he brings his right hand over the opponent's neck **(3)** and turns him around by grabbing and locking his opponent's attacking limb **(4)**. This action brings the opponent to the ground **(5)**, where Miyake finishes him off with a punch to the stomach **(6)**.

Detail #2

Reverse Angle

3

Detail #3

Reverse Angle

4

Detail #4

Reverse Angle

5

6

Miyake Sensei squares off against his opponent **(1)**. When the opponent attacks with a front kick, Miyake steps in and blocks with his right hand, simultaneously scoring with a front hand punch to the face **(2 & 3)**. Retreat to kamae. Zanchin **(4)**.

Sensei faces his opponent **(1)**. When the opponent attacks with a front kick, Miyake steps in, blocks with his right hand, and simultaneously scores with a front-hand punch to the face **(2)**. Then he grabs the opponent's leg with his right hand and controls the left shoulder with his left hand **(3)**.

Immediately, he turns his body to the left and unbalances his opponent **(4)**, which brings him onto the ground **(5)**, where Miyake finishes him off with a punch to the stomach **(6)**.

KUMITE RULES

In Karate, all matches are played under certain established rules. Naturally, there are certain limitations for karate techniques to be used in the match. The main limitations are as follows:

- "One on One" Limitation.
- Limited Targets.
- Limited Techniques.
- Limitations on Contest Area.
- Time Limitation.

As for other rules and limitations, the principles are set to make the most of Karate characteristics while carrying out the match with fairness and safety.

World Karate Federation

Kumite Rules

ARTICLE 1: KUMITE COMPETITION AREA

1. The competition area must be flat and devoid of hazard.

2. The competition area will be a matted square, with sides of eight meters (measured from the outside) with an additional two meters on all sides as a safety area. There will be a clear safety area of two meters on each side. The area may be elevated to a height of up to one meter above floor level. The elevated platform must measure at least twelve meters a side, in order to include both the competition and the safety areas.

3. A line half a meter long must be drawn two meters from the center of the competition area for positioning the Referee.

4. Two parallel lines each one meter long and at right angles to the Referee's line, must be drawn at a distance of one and a half meters from the center of the competition area for positioning the competitors.

5. The Judges will be seated in the safety area, one directly facing the referee, and one behind each of the fighters, and one meter towards the Referee. Each will be equipped with a red and a blue flag.

6. The Arbitrator will be seated at a small table just outside the safety area, behind, and to the left of the Referee. He will be equipped with a red flag or sign, and a buzzer.

7. The score-supervisor will be seated at the official score table, between the scorekeeper and the timekeeper.

8. The one meter border should be in a different color from the rest of the matted area.

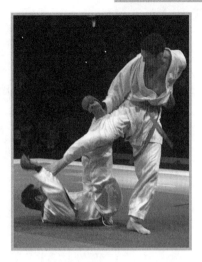

Explanation

I. There must be no advertisement hoardings, walls, pillars etc. within one meter of the safety area's outer perimeter.

II. The mats used should be non-slip where they contact the floor proper but have a low co-efficient of friction on the upper surface. They should not be as thick as Judo mats, since these impede Karate movement. The Referee must ensure that mat modules do not move apart during the competition, since gaps cause injuries and constitute a hazard. They must be of approved WKF design.

ARTICLE 2: OFFICIAL DRESS

1. Contestants and their coaches must wear the official uniform as herein defined.

2. The Referee Council may disbar any official or competitor who does not comply with this regulation.

Referees

1. Referees and Judges must wear the official uniform designated by the Referee Council. This uniform must be worn at all tournaments and courses.

2. The official uniform will be as follows:
   A single breasted navy blue blazer bearing two silver buttons.
   A white shirt with short sleeves.

An official tie, worn without tiepin.

Plain light-gray trousers without turn-ups.

Plain dark blue or black socks and black slip-on shoes for use on the match area.

Female referees and judges may wear a hairclip.

Contestants

1. Contestants must wear a white unmarked karate gi without stripes or piping. The national emblem or flag of the country may be worn on the left breast of the jacket and may not exceed an overall size of ten centimeters square (100mm by 100mm). Only the original manufacturer's labels may be displayed on the gi. In addition, an identifying number issued by the Organizing Committee may be worn on the back. One contestant must wear a red belt and the other a blue belt. The red and blue belts must be around five centimeters wide and of a length sufficient to allow fifteen centimeters free on each side of the knot.

2. Notwithstanding paragraph 1 above, the Directing Committee may authorize the display of special labels or trademarks of approved sponsors.

3. The jacket, when tightened around the waist with the belt, must be of a minimum length that covers the hips, but must not be more than three-quarters thigh length. Female competitors may wear a plain white T-shirt beneath the Karate jacket.

4. The maximum length of the jacket sleeves must be no longer then the bend of the wrist and no shorter than halfway down the forearm. Jacket sleeves may not be rolled up.

5. The trousers must be long enough to cover at least two thirds of the shin and must not reach below the anklebone. Trouser legs may not be rolled up.

6. Contestants must keep their hair clean and cut to a length that does not obstruct smooth bout conduct. Hachimaki (headband) will not be

allowed. Should the Referee consider any contestant's hair too long and/or unclean, he may disbar the contestant from the bout. In Kumite matches hair slides are prohibited, as are metal hairgrips. In Kata, a discreet hair clip is permitted. Ribbons and other decorations are prohibited.

7. Contestants must have short fingernails and must not wear metallic or other objects, which might injure their opponents. The use of metallic teeth braces must be approved by the Referee and the Official Doctor. The contestant accepts full responsibility for any injury.

8. WKF approved mitts, one contestant wearing red, and the other wearing blue are compulsory.

9. Gum shields are compulsory.

10. Boxes and soft shin pads are allowed. Shin/instep protectors are forbidden.

11. Glasses are forbidden. Soft contact lenses can be worn at the contestant's own risk.

12. The wearing of unauthorized clothing or equipment is forbidden. Women may wear the authorized additional protective equipment such as chest protectors.

13. All protective equipment must be W.K.F. homologated.

14. The use of bandages, padding, or supports because of injury must be approved by the Referee on the advice of the Official Doctor.

Coaches

1. The coach shall at all times during the tournament, wear a tracksuit and display official identification.

Explanation

I. The contestant must wear a single belt. This will be red for AKA and blue for AO. Belts of grade should not be worn during the bout.

II. Gum shields must fit properly. Groin protectors using a removable plastic cup slipped into a jockstrap are not permitted and persons wearing them will be held at fault.

III. There may well be a religious basis for the wearing of certain items such as turbans or amulets. Persons wishing, by virtue of their religion, to wear what would otherwise be construed as unauthorized clothing must notify the Referee Council in advance of a tournament. The Referee Council will examine each application on its merit. No accommodation will be made for people who just turn up on the day and expect to participate.

IV. If a contestant comes into the area inappropriately dressed, he or she will not be immediately disqualified; instead the fighter will be given one minute to remedy matters.

V. If the Referee Council agrees, Refereeing Officials may be allowed to remove their blazers.

ARTICLE 3: ORGANISATION OF KUMITE COMPETITIONS

1. A Karate tournament may comprise Kumite competition and/or Kata competition. The Kumite competition may be further divided into the team match and the individual match. The individual match may be further divided into weight divisions and open category. Weight divisions are divided ultimately into bouts. The term "bout" also describes the individual Kumite competitions between opposing pairs of team members.

2. No contestant may be replaced by another in an individual title match.

3. Individual contestants or teams that do not present themselves when called will be disqualified (KIKEN) from that category.

4. Male teams comprise seven members with five competing in a round. Female teams comprise four members with three competing in a round.

5. The contestants are all members of the team. There are no fixed reserves.

6. Before each match, a team repre-

sentative must hand into the official table, an official form defin-
ing the names and fighting order
of the competing team members.
The participants drawn from the
full team of seven, or four members, and their fighting order, can
be changed for each round provided the new fighting order is
notified first, but once notified, it
cannot then be changed until that
round is completed.

7. A team will be disqualified if any
   of its members or its coach
   changes the team's composition or fighting order without written notifi-
   cation prior to the round.

Explanation

I. A "round" is a discrete stage in a competition leading to the eventual
   identification of finalists. In an elimination Kumite competition, a round
   eliminates fifty percent of contestants within it, counting byes as contestants. In this context, the round can apply equally to a stage in either
   primary elimination or repechage. In a matrix, or "round robin" competition, a round allows all contestants in a pool to fight once.

II. The use of contestants' names causes problems of pronunciation and
    identification. Tournament numbers should be allotted and used.

III. When lining up before a match, a team will present the actual fighters.
     The unused fighter(s) and the Coach will not be included and shall sit in
     an area set aside for them.

IV. In order to compete male teams must present at least three competi-
    tors and female teams must present at least two competitors. A team
    with less than the required number of competitors will forfeit the match
    (Kiken).

V. The fighting order form can be presented by the Coach, or a nominated
   contestant from the team. If the Coach hands in the form, he must be
   clearly identifiable as such; otherwise, it may be rejected. The list must
   include the name of the country or club the belt color allotted to the

team for that match and the fighting order of the team members. Both the competitor's names and their tournament numbers must be included and the form signed by the coach, or a nominated person.

VI. If, through an error in charting, the wrong contestants compete, then regardless of the outcome, that bout/match is declared null and void. To reduce such errors the winner of each bout/match must confirm victory with the control table before leaving the area.

ARTICLE 4: THE REFEREE PANEL

1. The Refereeing Panel for each match shall consist of one Referee (SHUSHIN), three Judges (FUKUSHIN), and one arbitrator (KANSA).
2. The Referee and Judges of a Kumite bout must not have the nationality of either of the participants.
3. In addition, for facilitating the operation of matches, several timekeepers, caller announcers, record keepers, and score supervisors shall be appointed.

Explanation

I. At the start of a Kumite match, the Referee stands on the outside edge of the match area. On the Referee's left stand Judges numbers 1 and 2, and on the right stands the Arbitrator and Judge number 3.

II. After the formal exchange of bows by contestants and Referee Panel, the Referee takes a step back, the Judges and Arbitrator turn inwards, and all bow together. All then take up their positions.

III. When changing the entire Referee Panel, the departing Officials take up position as at the start of the bout or match, bow to each other, then leave the area together.

IV. When individual Judges change, the incoming Judge goes to the outgoing Judge, they bow together and change positions.

ARTICLE 5: DURATION OF BOUT

1. Duration of the Kumite bout is defined as three minutes for Senior Male Kumite (both teams and individuals) and two minutes for Women's, Junior, and Cadet bouts.
2. The timing of the bout starts when the Referee gives the signal to start, and stops each time the Referee calls "YAME".
3. The timekeeper shall give signals by a clearly audible gong, or buzzer, indicating "30 seconds to go" or "time up". The "time up" signal marks the end of the bout.

ARTICLE 6: SCORING

1. Scores are as follows:
   a) SANBON Three points
   b) NIHON Two points
   c) IPPON One point

2. A score is awarded when a technique is performed according to the following criteria to a scoring area:
   a) Good form
   b) Sporting attitude
   c) Vigorous application
   d) Awareness (ZANSHIN)
   e) Good timing
   f) Correct distance

3. SANBON is awarded for:
   a) Jodan kicks.
   b) Throwing or leg sweeping the opponent to the mat followed by a scoring technique.

4. NIHON is awarded for:
   a) Chudan kicks.
   b) Punches on the back., including back of the head and neck.

c) Combination hand techniques, the individual components of which each score in their own right.
d) Unbalancing the opponent and scoring.

5. IPPON is awarded for:
    a) Chudan or Jodan Tsuki.
    b) Uchi.

6. Attacks are limited to the following areas:
    a) Head
    b) Face
    c) Neck
    d) Abdomen
    e) Chest
    f) Back
    g) Side

7. An effective technique delivered at the same time that the end of the bout is signaled, is considered valid. A technique even if effective, delivered after an order to suspend or stop the bout shall not be scored and may result in a penalty being imposed on the offender.

8. No technique, even if technically correct, will be scored if it is delivered when the two contestants are outside the competition area. However, if

one of the contestants delivers an effective technique while still inside the competition area and before the Referee calls "YAME", the technique will be scored.

9. Simultaneous, effective scoring techniques delivered by both contestants, the one on the other (AIUCHI) shall not score.

Explanation

I. In order to score, a technique must be applied to a scoring area as defined in paragraph 6 above.

The technique must be appropriately controlled with regard to the area being attacked and must satisfy all six scoring criteria in paragraph 2 above.

Technical Criteria

Sanbon (3 Points) is awarded for:

* Jodan kicks. Jodan being defined as the face, head and neck.

* Any scoring technique which is delivered after legally throwing, leg sweeping, or taking the opponent down to the mat.

Nihon (2 Points) is awarded for:

* Chudan kicks. Chudan being defined as the abdomen, chest, back and side.

* Punches delivered to the opponent's back, including the back of the head and neck.

* Combinations of punching and striking (tsuki and uchi) the individual components of which each score in their own right, delivered to any of the seven scoring areas.

* Any scoring technique delivered after permissible physical action of the contestant has caused the opponent to lose balance as the score is made.

Ippon (1 Point) is awarded for:

* Any punch (tsuki) delivered to any of the seven scoring areas excluding the back, the back of the head and neck.

* Any strike (uchi) delivered to any of the seven scoring areas.

I. For reasons of safety, throws where the opponent is thrown without being held onto, or thrown dangerously, or where the pivot point is above hip level, are prohibited and will incur a warning or penalty. Exceptions are conventional karate leg sweeping techniques, which do not require the opponent to be held while executing the sweep such as

de ashi-barai, kouchi-gari, kani-waza etc. After a throw has been executed the referee will allow the contestant two to three seconds in which to attempt a scoring technique.

II. When a contestant slips, falls, or loses balance as a result of their own action and is scored upon by the opponent the score will be given as if the contestant had been standing upright.

III. A technique with "Good Form" is said to have characteristics conferring probable effectiveness within the framework of traditional Karate concepts.

IV. Sporting Attitude is a component of good form and refers to a non-malicious attitude of great concentration obvious during delivery of the scoring technique.

V. Vigorous Application defines the power and speed of the technique and the palpable will for it to succeed.

VI. Awareness (ZANSHIN) is that criterion most often missed when a score is assessed. It is the state of continued commitment in which the contestant maintains total concentration, observation, and awareness of the opponent's potentiality to counter-attack. He does not turn his face away during delivery of the technique, and remains facing the opponent afterwards.

VII. Good Timing means delivering a technique when it will have the greatest potential effect.

VIII. Correct Distance similarly means delivering a technique at the precise distance where it will have the greatest potential effect. Thus if the technique is delivered on an opponent who is rapidly moving away, the potential effect of that blow is reduced.

IX. Distancing also relates to the point at which the completed technique comes to rest on or near the target. A punch or kick that comes somewhere between skin touch and 2—5 centimetres from the face, may be said to have the correct distance. However, Jodan punches, which come within a reasonable distance of the target and which the opponent makes no attempt to block or avoid will be scored, provided the technique meets the other criteria.

X.   A worthless technique is a worthless technique—regardless of where and how it is delivered. A technique, which is badly deficient in good form, or lacking power, will score nothing.

XI. Techniques, which land below the belt may score, as long as they are above the pubic bone. The neck is a target area and so is the throat. However, no contact to the throat is permitted, although a score may be awarded for a properly controlled technique, which does not touch.

XII. A technique, which lands upon the shoulder blades, may score. The non-scoring part of the shoulder is the junction of the upper bone of the arm with the shoulder blades and collarbones.

XIII. The time-up bell signals the end of scoring possibilities in that bout, even though the Referee may inadvertently not halt the bout immediately. The time-up bell does not however mean that penalties cannot be imposed. Penalties can be imposed by the Refereeing Panel up to the point where the contestants leave that area after the bout's conclusion. Penalties can be imposed after that, but then only by the Referee Council.

XIV. True Aiuchi are rare. Not only must two techniques land simultaneously, but both must be valid scoring techniques, each with good form etc. Two techniques may well land simultaneously, but seldom are both, if indeed either, effective scores. The Referee must not dismiss as Aiuchi, a situation where only one of the simultaneous pair is actually a score. This is not Aiuchi.

ARTICLE 7: CRITERIA FOR DECISION

The result of a bout is determined by a contestant obtaining a clear lead of eight points, or at time-up, having the highest number of points, obtaining a decision (HANTEI), or by a HANSOKU, SHIKKAKU, or KIKEN, imposed against a contestant.

1. When a bout ends with equal scores, or no scores, the Referee will announce a tie (HIKIWAKE) and the start of the ENCHO-SEN if applicable.
2. In individual bouts, if there is a tie, an extension not exceeding one minute will be fought (ENCHO-SEN). An ENCHO-SEN is an extension of the bout, and all penalties and warnings issued still apply. The first competitor to obtain an award will be declared the winner. In the event that neither competitor is awarded a score, during the ENCHO-SEN, the decision will be made by a final vote of the Referee and three Judges (HANTEI). A decision in favor of one or the other competitor is obligatory and is taken on the basis of the following;
    a) The attitude, fighting spirit, and strength demonstrated by the contestants.
    b) The superiority of tactics and techniques displayed.
    c) Which of the contestants has initiated the majority of the action.
3. In team competition, there will be no extension (ENCHO-SEN) in the event of drawn bouts except as stated in paragraph 5 below.
4. The winning team is the one with the most bout victories. Should the two teams have the same number of bout victories then the winning

team will be the one with the most points, taking both winning and losing bouts into account.

5. If the two teams have the same number of bout victories and points, then a deciding bout will be held. In the event of a continuing tie, there will be an extension (ENCHO-SEN) not exceeding one minute. The first competitor to obtain an award will be declared the winner. In the event that there is no score the decision will be made by vote of the Referee and three Judges (HANTEI).

6. In team matches when a team, has won sufficient bout victories or scored sufficient points as to be the established winner then the match is declared over and no further bouts will take place.

Explanation

I. When deciding the outcome of a bout by vote (HANTEI) at the end of an inconclusive ENCHO-SEN, the Referee will move to the match area perimeter and call "HANTEI", followed by a two-tone blast of the whistle. The Judges will indicate their opinions by means of their flags and the Referee will at the same time indicate his own vote by raising his arm on the side of the preferred contestant. The Referee will give a short blast on his whistle, return to his original position and announce the majority decision.

II. In the event of a tied vote, the Referee will resolve the tie by use of his casting vote. On returning to his original position, the Referee will place one arm across his chest and raise his bent arm on the side of the preferred choice to show he is using his casting vote. He will then indicate the winner in the normal way

ARTICLE 8: PROHIBITED BEHAVIOUR

There are two categories of prohibited behavior, Category 1 and Category 2.

Category 1

1. Techniques which make excessive contact, having regard to the scoring area attacked, and techniques which make contact with the throat.
2. Attacks to the arms or legs, groin, joints, or instep.
3. Attacks to the face with open hand techniques.
4. Dangerous or forbidden throwing techniques.

Category 2

1. Feigning, or exaggerating injury.
2. Repeated exits from the competition area (JOGAI).

3. Self-endangerment by indulging in behavior, which exposes the contestant to injury by the opponent, or failing to take adequate measures for self-protection, (MUBOBI).

4. Avoiding combat as a means of preventing the opponent having the opportunity to score.

5. Clinching, wrestling, pushing, or seizing, without attempting a throw or other technique.

6. Techniques, which by their nature, cannot be controlled for the safety of the opponent and dangerous and uncontrolled attacks.

7. Attacks with the head, knees, or elbows.

8. Talking to, or goading the opponent, failing to obey the orders of the referee, discourteous behavior towards the refereeing officials, or other breaches of etiquette.

Explanation

I. Karate competition is a sport, and for that reason some of the most dangerous techniques are banned and all techniques must be controlled. Trained competitors can absorb relatively powerful blows on muscled areas such as the abdomen, but the fact remains that the head, face, neck, groin and joints are particularly susceptible to injury. Therefore any technique, which results in injury, may be penalized unless caused by the recipient. The contestants must perform all techniques with control and good form. If they cannot, then regardless of the technique misused, a warning or penalty must be imposed.

Face Contact—Seniors and Juniors

II. For Senior and Junior competitors, non-injurious, light, controlled "touch" contact to the face, head, and neck is allowed (but not to the throat). Where contact is deemed by the referee to be too strong, but does not diminish the competitor's chances of winning, a warning (CHUKOKU) may be given. A second contact under the same circumstances will be penalized by KEIKOKU and IPPON (one point), given to the opponent. A third offence will be given HANSOKU CHUI and NIHON (two points), to the injured competitor. A further offence will result in disqualification by HANSOKU.

Face Contact—Cadets

III.   For Cadets, all hand techniques to the head, face, and neck must have absolute control. Should the glove touch the target the Referee Panel will not award a score. Kicking techniques to the head, face and neck, are allowed to make a light "skin touch" only. In the case of techniques, which make contact considered to be more than a "glove" or "skin" touch, the Referee Panel will give a warning or penalty. Any technique to the head, face or neck, which causes injury no matter how slight, will be warned or penalized unless caused by the recipient.

IV.   The Referee must constantly observe the injured contestant. A short delay in giving a judgment allows injury symptoms such as a nose-bleed to develop. Observation will also reveal any efforts by the contestant to aggravate slight injury for tactical advantage. Examples of this are blowing violently through an injured nose, or rubbing the face roughly.

V.   Pre-existing injury can produce symptoms out of all proportion to the degree of contact used and referees must take this into account when considering penalties for seemingly excessive contact. For example, what appears to be a relatively light contact could result in a competitor being unable to continue due to the cumulative effect of injury sustained in an earlier bout. Before the start of a match or bout, the Match Area Controller must examine the medical cards

and ensure that the contestants are fit to fight. The Referee must be informed if a contestant has been treated for injury.

VI.   Contestants who over-react to light contact, in an effort to have the referee penalize their opponent, such as holding the face and staggering about, or falling unnecessarily, will be immediately warned or penalized themselves.

VII.   Feigning of an injury, which does not exist, is a serious infraction of the rules. SHIKKAKU will be imposed on the contestant feigning injury i.e., when such things as collapse and rolling about on the floor are not supported by evidence of commensurate injury as reported by a neutral doctor. Exaggerating an injury, which does exist is less serious. A warning or penalty should be imposed for exaggerating injury.

VIII. Competitors, who receive SHIKKAKU for feigning injury will be taken from the competition area and put directly into the hands of the W.K.F. Medical Commission, who will carry out an immediate examination of the competitor. The Medical Commission will submit its report before the end of the Championship, for the consideration of the Referee Council. Competitors who feign injury will be subject to the strongest penalties, up to and including suspension for life for repeated offences.

IX.   The throat is a particularly vulnerable area and even the slightest contact will be warned or penalized, unless it is the recipient's own fault.

X.   Throwing techniques are divided into two types. The established "conventional" karate leg sweeping techniques such as de ashi-barai,

kouchi-gari, etc., where the opponent is swept off-balance or thrown without being grabbed first—and those throws requiring that the opponent be grabbed or held as the throw is executed. The pivotal point of the throw must not be above the hip and the opponent must be held onto throughout, so that a safe landing can be made. Over the shoulder throws such as seio-nage, kata garuma etc., are expressly forbidden, as are so-called "sacrifice" throws such as tomoe-nage, sumi-gaeshi etc. If an opponent is injured as a result of a throwing technique, the Referee Panel will decide whether a penalty is called for.

XI. Open hand techniques to the face are forbidden due to the danger to the contestant's sight.

XII. JOGAI relates to a situation where a contestant's foot, or any other part of the body, touches the floor outside of the match area. An exception is when the contestant is physically pushed or thrown from the area by the opponent.

XIII. A contestant who delivers a scoring technique then exits the area before the Referee calls "Yamae" will be given the value of the score and Jogai will not be imposed. If the contestant's attempt to score is unsuccessful the exit will be recorded as a Jogai.

XIV. If AO exits just after Aka scores with a successful attack, then "Yame" will occur immediately on the score and AO's exit will not be recorded. If AO exits, or has exited as Aka's score is made (with Aka remaining within the area), then both Aka's score will be awarded and AO's Jogai penalty will be imposed.

XV. The contestant who constantly retreats without effective counter, who clinches unnecessarily, or who deliberately exits the area rather than allow the opponent an opportunity to score must be warned or penalized. This often occurs during the closing seconds of a bout. If the offence occurs with ten seconds or more of the bout time remaining the referee will warn the offender. If there has been a previous Category 2 offence or offences, this will result in a penalty being imposed.

If however, there is less than ten seconds to go, the referee will penalize the offender with Keikoku (whether there has been a previ-

ous Category 2 Chukoku or not) and award an Ippon to the opponent. If there has been a previous Category 2 Keikoku the Referee will penalise the offender with Hansoku Chui and award Nihon to the opponent. If there has been a previous Category 2 Hansoku Chui the Referee will penalize the offender with Hansoku and award the bout to the opponent. However, the referee must ensure that the contestant's behavior is not a defensive measure due to the opponent acting in a reckless or dangerous manner, in which case the attacker should be warned or penalized.

XVI. An example of MUBOBI is the instance in which the contestant launches a committed attack without regard for personal safety. Some contestants throw themselves into a long reverse-punch, and are unable to block a counter. Such open attacks constitute an act of Mubobi and cannot score. As a tactical theatrical move, some fighters turn away immediately in a mock display of dominance to demonstrate a scored point. They drop their guard and lapse awareness of the opponent. The purpose of the turn-away is to draw the Referee's attention to their technique. This is also a clear act of Mubobi. Should the offender receive an excessive contact and/or sustain an injury and the fault is considered to be the recipient's, the referee will issue a Category 2 warning or penalty and may decline to give a penalty to the opponent.

XVII. Any discourteous behavior from a member of an official delegation can earn the disqualification of a competitor, the entire team, or delegation from the tournament.

ARTICLE 9: PENALTIES

WARNING: (CHUKOKU): May be imposed for attendant minor infractions or the first instance of a minor infraction.

KEIKOKU: This is a penalty in which IPPON (one point), is added to the opponent's score. KEIKOKU is imposed for minor infractions for which a warning has previously been given in that bout, or for infractions not sufficiently serious to merit HANSOKU-CHUI.

HANSOKU-CHUI: This is a penalty in which NIHON (two points), is added to the opponent's score. HANSOKU-CHUI is usually imposed for infractions for which a KEIKOKU has previously been given in that bout although it may be imposed directly for serious infringements, which do not merit HANSOKU.

HANSOKU: This is imposed following a very serious infraction or when a HANSOKU CHUI has already been given. It results in the disqualification of the contestant. In team matches the fouled competitor's score will be set at eight points and the offender's score will be zeroed.

SHIKKAKU: This is a disqualification from the actual tournament, competition, or match In order to define the limit of SHIKKAKU, the Referee Council, must be consulted. SHIKKAKU may be invoked when a contestant fails to obey the orders of the referee, acts maliciously, or commits an act which harms the prestige and honor of Karate-do, or when other actions are considered to violate the rules and spirit of the tournament. In team matches the fouled competitor's score will be set at eight points and the offender's score will be zeroed.

Explanation

I.   Category 1 and Category 2 penalties do not cross-accumulate.

II. A penalty can be directly imposed for a rules infraction but once given, repeats of that category of infraction must be accompanied by an increase in severity of penalty imposed. It is not, for example, possible to give a warning or penalty for excessive

contact then give another warning for a second instance of excessive contact.

III. Warnings (CHUKOKU) are given where there has clearly been a minor infraction of the rules, but the contestant's potential for winning is not diminished (in the opinion of the Referee Panel) by the opponent's foul.

IV. A KEIKOKU may be imposed directly, without first giving a warning. KEIKOKU is normally imposed where the contestant's potential for winning is slightly diminished (in the opinion of the Referee Panel) by the opponent's foul.

V. A HANSOKU CHUI may be imposed directly, or following a warning, or KEIKOKU and is used where the contestant's potential for winning has been seriously reduced (in the opinion of the Referee Panel) by the opponent's foul.

VI. A HANSOKU is imposed for cumulative penalties but can also be imposed directly for serious rules infractions. It is used when the contestant's potential for winning has been reduced virtually to zero (in the opinion of the Referee Panel) by the opponent's foul.

VII. Any competitor who receives HANSOKU for causing injury, and who has in the opinion of the Referee Panel and Match Area Controller,

acted recklessly or dangerously or who is considered not to have the requisite control skills necessary for WKF competition, will be reported to the Referee Council. The Referee Council will decide if that competitor shall be suspended from the rest of that competition and/or subsequent competitions.

VIII. A SHIKKAKU can be directly imposed, without warnings of any kind. The contestant need have done nothing to merit it—it is sufficient if the Coach or non-combatant members of the contestants' delegation behave in such a way as to harm the prestige and honor of Karate-Do. If the Referee believes that a contestant has acted maliciously, regardless of whether or not actual physical injury has been caused, Shikkaku and not Hansoku, is the correct penalty.

IX.   A public announcement of Shikkaku must be made

ARTICLE 10: INJURIES AND ACCIDENTS IN COMPETITION

1.   KIKEN or forfeiture is the decision given, when a contestant or contestants fail to present themselves when called, are unable to continue, abandon the bout, or are withdrawn on the order of the Referee. The grounds for abandonment may include injury not ascribable to the opponent's actions.

2.   If two contestants injure each other, or are suffering from the effects of previously incurred injury, and are declared by the tournament doctor to be unable to continue, the bout is awarded to the contestant who has amassed the most points. In Individual Matches if the points score is equal, then a vote (HANTEI) will decide the outcome of the bout. In Team Matches the Referee will announce a tie (HIKIWAKE). Should the situation occur in a deciding Team Match ENCHO-SEN then a vote (HANTEI) will determine the outcome.

3.   An injured contestant who has been declared unfit to fight by the tournament doctor cannot fight again in that competition.

4.   An injured contestant who wins a bout through disqualification due to injury is not allowed to fight again in the competition without permission from the doctor. If he is injured, he may win a second bout by disqualification but is immediately withdrawn from further Kumite competition in that tournament.

5. When a contestant is injured, the Referee shall at once halt the bout and call the doctor. The doctor is authorized to diagnose and treat injury only.

6. A competitor who is injured during a bout in progress and requires medical treatment will be allowed three minutes in which to receive it. If treatment is not completed within the time allowed, the Referee will decide if the competitor shall be declared unfit to fight (Article 13, Paragraph 9d), or whether an extension of treatment time shall be given.

7. Any competitor who falls, is thrown, or knocked down, and does not fully regain his or her feet within ten seconds, is considered unfit to continue fighting and will be automatically withdrawn from all Kumite events in that tournament. In the event that a competitor falls, is thrown, or knocked down and does not regain his or her feet immediately, the referee will signal to the timekeeper to start the ten second count-down by a blast on his whistle, at the same time calling the doctor if required. The time-keeper will stop the clock when the referee raises his arm.

EXPLANATION:

I.   When the doctor declares the contestant unfit, the appropriate entry must be made on the contestant's monitoring card. The extent of unfitness must be made clear to other Refereeing Panels.

II. A contestant may win through disqualification of the opponent for accumulated minor Category 1 infractions. Perhaps the winner has sustained no significant injury. A second win on the same grounds must lead to withdrawal, even though the contestant may be physically able to continue.

III. The referee should only call the doctor when a contestant is injured and needs medical treatment.

IV.   The doctor is obliged to make safety recommendations only as they relate to the proper medical management of that particular injured contestant.

V.   When applying the "Ten Second Rule" the time will be kept by a time-keeper appointed for this specific purpose. A warning will be sounded at seven seconds followed by the final bell at ten seconds. The time-keeper will start the clock only on the referee's signal. The time-keeper will stop the clock when the competitor stands fully upright and the referee raises his arm.

VI.   The Referee Panel will decide the winner on the basis of HANSOKU, KIKEN, or SHIKKAKU as the case may be.

VII.   In team matches, should a team member receive KIKEN, their score, if any, will be zeroed and the opponent's score will be set at eight points.

ARTICLE 11: OFFICIAL PROTEST

1.   No one may protest about a judgment to the members of the Refereeing Panel.

2.   If a refereeing procedure appears to contravene the rules, the President of the Federation, or the official representative is the only one allowed to make a protest.

3.   The protest will take the form of a written report submitted immediately after the bout in which the protest was generated. (The sole exception is when the protest concerns an administrative malfunction. The Match Area Controller should be notified immediately the administrative malfunction is detected).

4. The protest must be submitted to a representative of the Appeals Jury. In due course the Jury will review the circumstances leading to the protested decision. Having considered all the facts available, they will produce a report, and shall be empowered to take such action as may be called for.

5. Any protest concerning application of the rules must be made in accordance with the complaints procedure defined by the WKF DC. It must be submitted in writing and signed by the official representative of the team or contestant(s).

6. The complainant must deposit a Protest Fee as agreed by the WKF DC, and this, together with the protest must be lodged with a representative of the Appeals Jury.

7. The Appeals Jury is comprised of one representative each from the Referee Council, Technical Committee, and Medical Committee.

Explanation

I. The protest must give the names of the contestants, the Referee Panel officiating, and the precise details of what is being protested. No general claims about overall standards will be accepted as a legitimate protest. The burden of proving the validity of the protest lies with the complainant.

II. The protest will be reviewed by the Appeals Jury and as part of this review, the Jury will study the evidence submitted in support of the protest. The Jury may also study videos and question Officials, in an effort to objectively examine the protest's validity.

III. If the protest is held by the Appeals Jury to be valid, the appropriate action will be taken. In addition, all such measures will be taken to

avoid a recurrence in future competitions. The deposit paid will be refunded by the Treasury.

IV. If the protest is held by the Appeals Jury to be invalid, it will be rejected and the deposit forfeited to WKF.

V. Ensuing matches or bouts will not be delayed, even if an official protest is being prepared. It is the responsibility of the Arbitrator, to ensure that the match has been conducted in accordance with the Rules of Competition.

VI. In case of an administrative malfunction during a match in progress, the Coach can notify the Match Area Controller directly. In

turn, the Match Area Controller will
notify the Referee.

ARTICLE 12: POWERS AND DUTIES

Referee Council

The Referee Council's powers and duties
shall be as follows:

1. To ensure the correct preparation for
    each given tournament in consultation
    with the Organizing Committee, with
    regard to competition area arrangement,
    the provision and deployment of all
    equipment and necessary facilities,
    match operation and supervision, safety
    precautions, etc.
2. To appoint and deploy the Match Area Controllers (Chief Referees) to
    their respective areas and to act upon and take such action as may be
    required by the reports of the Match Area Controllers.
3. To supervise and co-ordinate the overall performance of the refereeing
    officials.
4. To nominate substitute officials where such are required.
5. To pass the final judgment on matters of a technical nature which may
    arise during a given match and for which there are no stipulations in
    the rules.

Match Area Controllers

1. The Match Area Controllers powers and duties shall be as follows:
2. To delegate, appoint, and supervise the Referees and Judges, for all
    matches in areas under their control.
3. To oversee the performance of the Referees and Judges in their areas,
    and to ensure that the Officials appointed are capable of the tasks allot-
    ted them.
4. To order the Referee to halt the match when the Arbitrator signals a
    contravention of the Rules of Competition.
5. To prepare a daily, written report, on the performance of each official
    under their supervision, together with their recommendations, if any, to
    the Referee Council.

Referees

The Referee's powers shall be as follows:

1. The Referee ("SHUSHIN") shall have the power to conduct matches including announcing the start, the suspension, and the end of the match.

2. To award points.

3. To explain to the Match Area Controller, Referee Council, or Appeals Jury, if necessary, the basis for giving a judgment.

4. To impose penalties and to issue warnings, before, during, or after a bout.

5. To obtain and act upon the opinion(s) of the Judges.

6. To announce extensions.

7. To conduct voting of the Referee Panel (HANTEI) and announce the result.

8. To announce the winner.

9. The authority of the Referee is not confined solely to the competition area but also to all of its immediate perimeter.

10. The Referee shall give all commands and make all announcements.

Judges

The Judges (FUKUSHIN) powers shall be as follows:

1 To assist the Referee by flag signals.

2. To exercise a right to vote on a decision to be taken.

The Judges shall carefully observe the actions of the contestants and signal to the Referee an opinion in the following cases:

a) When a score is observed.

b) When a contestant has committed a prohibited act and/or techniques.

c) When an injury or illness of a contestant is noticed.

d) When both or either of the contestants have moved out of the competition area (JOGAI).

e) In other cases when it is deemed necessary to call the attention of the Referee.

Arbitrators

The Arbitrator (KANSA) will assist the Match Area Controller by overseeing the match or bout in progress. Should decisions of the Referee and/or Judges, not be in accordance with the Rules of Competition, the Arbitrator will immediately raise the red flag or sign and sound the buzzer. The Match Area Controller will instruct the Referee to halt the match or bout and correct the irregularity. Records kept of the match shall become official records subject to the approval of the Arbitrator.

Score Supervisors

The Score Supervisor will keep a separate record of the scores awarded by the Referee and at the same time oversee the actions of the appointed timekeepers and scorekeepers.

Explanation

I.   When three judges give the same signal, or indicate a score for the same competitor, the referee will stop the bout and render the majority decision. Should the referee fail to stop the bout the arbitrator will raise the red flag or sign and sound the buzzer.

II. When two judges give the same signal, or indicate a score for the same competitor, the referee will consider their opinions but may decline to stop the bout if he believes them to be mistaken.

III. However, when the bout is halted, the majority decision will prevail. The referee may ask the judges to re-consider, but may not give a decision against two judges, unless he has the positive support of the other judge.

IV. When the Referee sees a score he will call "YAME" and halt the bout using the prescribed signal. He will then indicate his preference by holding his bent arm palm upwards on the side of the scoring contestant.

V.   In the event of a two/two decision the Referee will indicate with the appropriate signal why the other contestant's score is not considered to be valid and then award the score to the opponent.

VI. The referee may ask the judges to re-consider when he believes them mistaken, or when implementation would be a violation of the rules.

VII. When three judges each have different opinions, the referee may give a decision, which is supported by one of the judges.

VIII. At HANTEI the referee and judges each have one vote. In the event of a tied ENCHO-SEN the Referee will have a casting vote.

IX. The Judges must only score what they actually see. If they are not sure that a technique actually reached a scoring area, they should signal that they did not see, (MIENAI).

X. The role of the Arbitrator is to ensure that the match or bout is conducted in accordance with the Rules of Competition. He is not there as an additional Judge. He has no vote, nor has he any authority in matters of judgment, such as whether a score was valid or if JOGAI occurred. His sole responsibility is in matters of procedure.

XI. In the event that the Referee does not hear the time-up bell, the Score-Supervisor will blow his whistle.

XII. When explaining the basis for a judgment after the match, the Referee Panel may speak to the Match Area Controller, the Referee Council, or the Appeals Jury. They will explain to no one else.

ARTICLE 13: STARTING, SUSPENDING AND ENDING OF MATCHES

1. The terms and gestures to be used by the Referee and Judges in the operation of a match shall be as specified in Appendices 1 and 2.

2. The Referee and Judges shall take up their prescribed positions and following an exchange of bows between the contestants; the Referee will announce "SHOBU HAJIME!" and the bout will commence.

3. The Referee will stop the bout by announcing "YAME". If necessary, the Referee will order the contestants to take

up their original positions (MOTO NO ICHI).

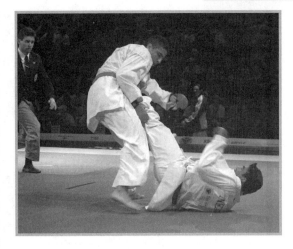

4. The Referee returns to his position and the Judges indicate their opinion by means of a signal. In the case of a score to be awarded the Referee identifies the contestant (Aka or AO), the area attacked (Chudan or Jodan), the scoring technique (Tsuki, Uchi, or Keri), and then awards the relevant score using the prescribed gesture. The Referee then restarts the bout by calling "TSUZUKETE HAJIME."

5. When a contestant has established a clear lead of eight points during a bout, the Referee shall call "YAME" and order the contestants back to their starting lines as he returns to his. The winner is then declared and indicated by the Referee raising a hand on the side of the winner and declaring "AO (AKA) NO KACHI". The bout is ended at this point.

6. When time is up, the contestant who has the most points is declared the winner, indicated by the Referee raising a hand on the side of the winner, and declaring "AO (AKA) NO KACHI". The bout is ended at this point.

7. When time is up and scores are equal, or no scores have been awarded, the Referee shall call "YAME" and return to his position. He will announce a tie (HIKIWAKE) and start the ENCHO-SEN if applicable.

8. At HANTEI the Referee and Judges each have one vote. In the event of a tied vote at the end of an inconclusive ENCHO-SEN the Referee will have a casting vote which will be used to break the tie.

9. When faced with the following situations, the Referee will call "YAME!" and halt the bout temporarily.
   a. When either or both contestants are out of the match area.
   b. When the Referee orders the contestant to adjust the karate- gi or protective equipment.
   c. When a contestant has contravened the rules.
   d. When the Referee considers that one or both of the contestants cannot continue with the bout owing to injuries, illness, or other

causes. Heeding the tournament doctor's opinion, the Referee will decide whether the bout should be continued.

e. When a contestant seizes the opponent and does not perform an immediate technique, or throw within two to three seconds.

f. When one or both contestants fall or are thrown and no effective techniques are made within two to three seconds.

g. When both contestants are off their feet following a fall or attempted throw and begin to wrestle.

h.   When a score is observed.

i.   When three judges give the same signal, or indicate a score for the same competitor.

j.   When requested to do so by the Match Area Controller.

Explanation

I.   When beginning a bout, the Referee first calls the contestants to their starting lines. If a contestant enters the area prematurely, they must be motioned off. The contestants must bow properly to each other—a quick nod is both discourteous and insufficient. The Referee can call for a bow where none is volunteered by motioning as shown in Appendix 2 of the rules.

II. When restarting the bout, the Referee should check that both contestants are on their lines and properly composed. Contestants jumping up and down or otherwise fidgeting must be stilled before combat can recommence. The Referee must restart the bout with the minimum of delay.

ARTICLE 14: MODIFICATIONS

Only the WKF Sports Commission with the approval of the WKF Directing Committee can alter or modify these rules.

EPILOGUE

Now that you have finished this book, what have you learned?

Hopefully, nothing less than a series of practical and efficient techniques for becoming a successful karate practitioner. These techniques will help you to succeed in competition and learn and grow after each defeat. These techniques have been developed by world-class competitors who have successfully applied them in elite competition. By using the same methods, you can also enjoy success in your matches, even if you are not a world-class competitor. But simply reading through these pages is not enough. You must consistently practice each technique with a training partner, exploring all the possibilities of each movement, until you obtain the desired results based on your body style, athletic ability and physical attributes. Not all these techniques will work for every karate-ka.

Once you have a basic framework in place, you must fine-tune each technique until it fits your game. The enjoyable part of the kumite aspect of karate-do is that everyone can adapt and personalize it. While the basics are the same, the application of the basics is as different and varied as each practitioner. When practiced under the guidance of an instructor, or with the assistance of a willing training partner, the techniques, principles and methods explained in this book will be effective, because they have been tested and proven in the laboratory of practical experience and the crucible of real competition.

Your task now is simple; go out and have fun with them!

—The authors

Winning Kumite